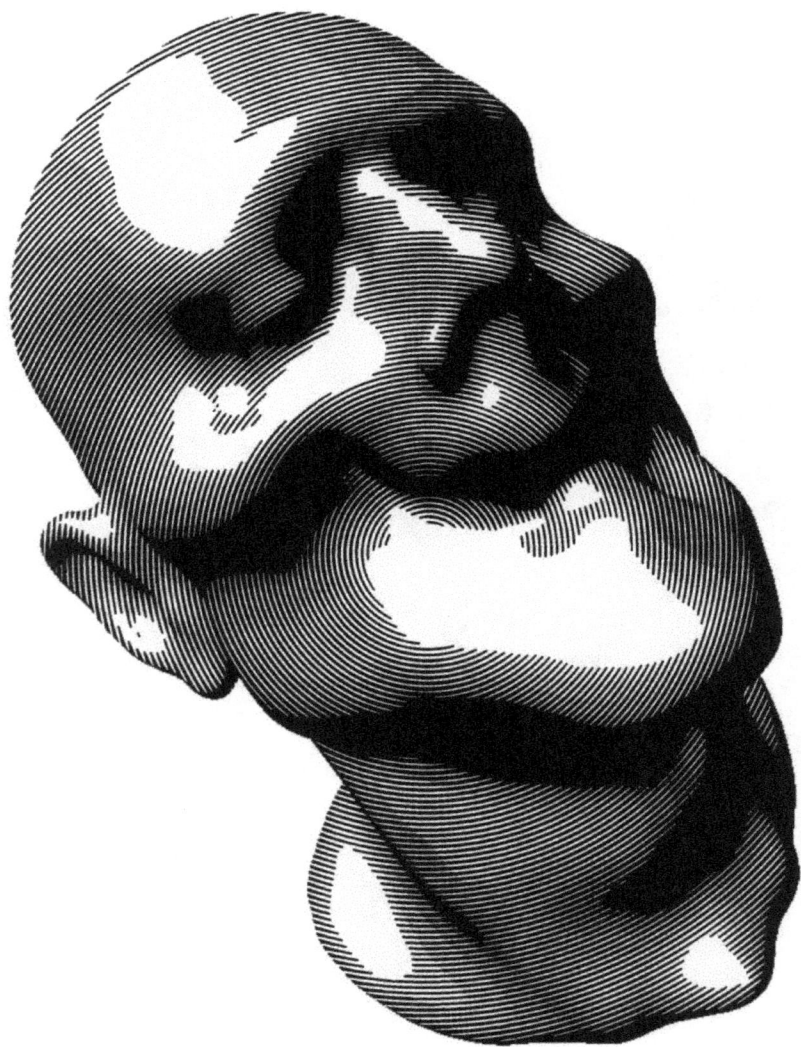

CORY ALLEN   DANIEL EDWARDS

THIS IS

Maybe....

AN

EVENT

EDITED BY
AMBER LOSSON

Visit our Web site at www.appleparrot.com

Cover design by Daniel Edwards
Book design by Cory Allen

AppleParrot Halftime Special poems and haiku used by
permission of Carey Bell and August Edwards.

ISBN-10:0-61545037-7
ISBN-13:978-0-6154-5037-7

10 9 8 7 6 5 4 3 2 1

First Edition

for Trae

The world is yours...take it!

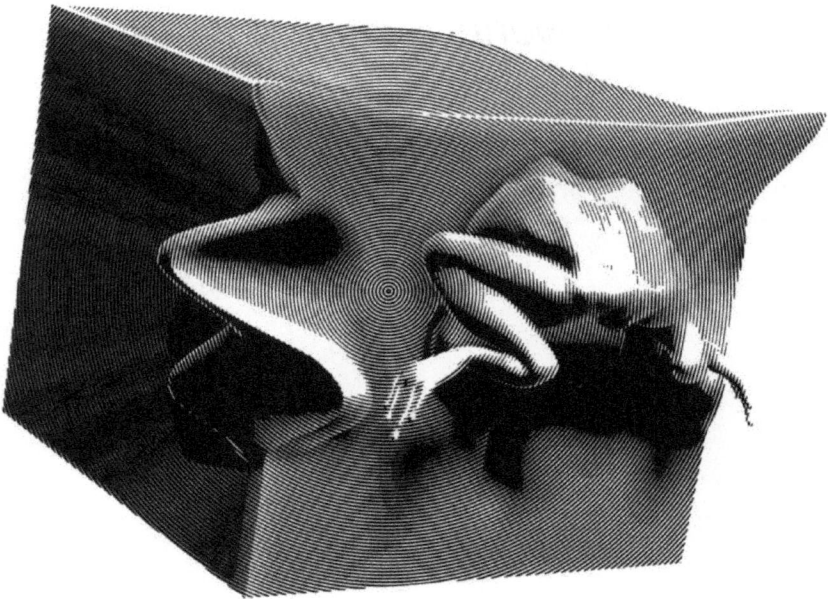

introduction

I knew once I completed *Maybe*
I would have to conclude
with an introduction...

Table of Contents

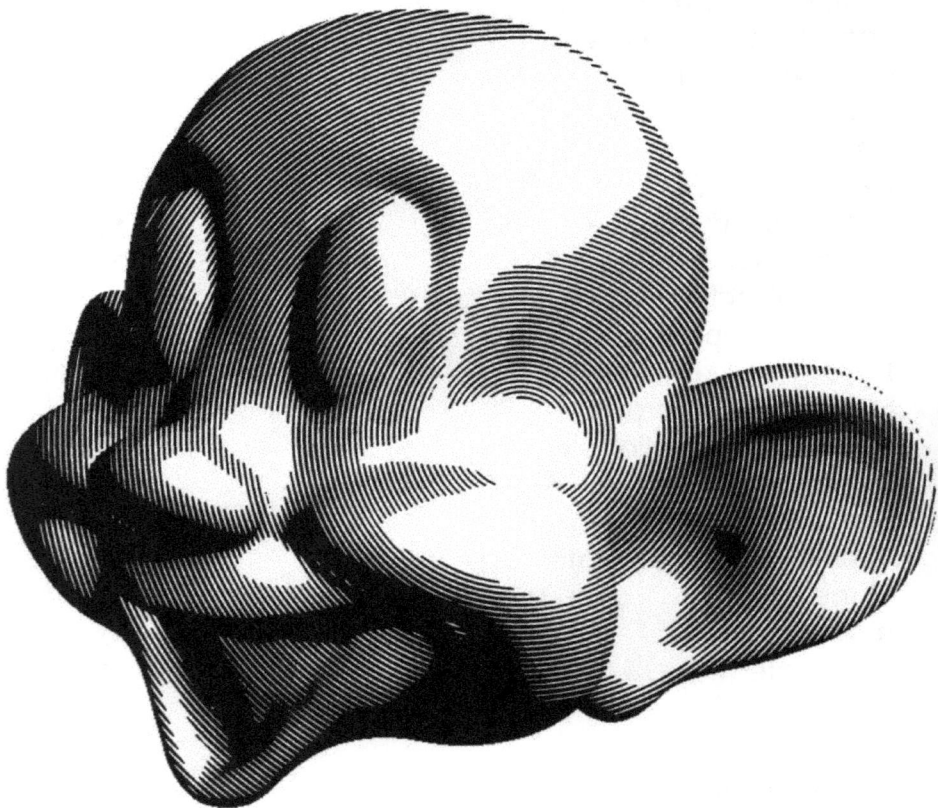

an important message

I'm not here right now
BUT
if you leave your
name
number
and a brief message
I'll get back to you
as soon as I can.

thank you

AND

have a nice day.

ask your doctor: anti-anti

this error stands before us
and
i'm not away...i have instituted a way
to disconnect
my thoughts for any given regimen
the turbulence of day-to-day
routines and politics...ignorance
the embedded intellects
commercializing my self-esteem...my smile
BUT they don't know who I am
i'm no longer listed in the phone book

smoking kills...
as does conversation in a civilized society
false advertising
their prescribed antics give nothing
BUT shared side effects
til death do us part
as long as you both shall live
raise your right hand
AND swear...
god damn it! SWEAR!

warning
this may cause diarrhea
and i no longer give a shit

fast food

please
drive
through

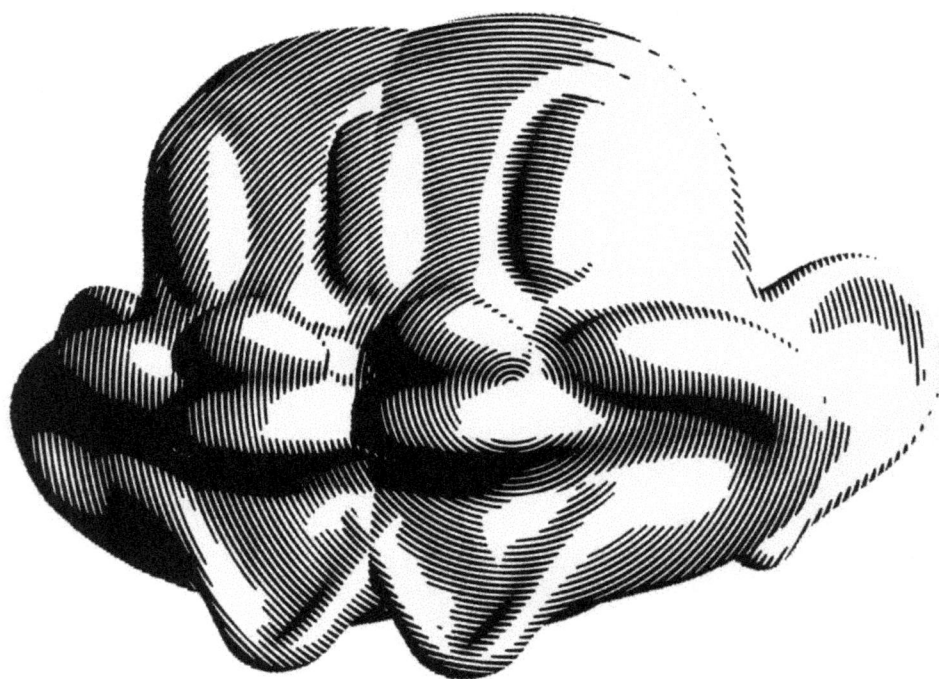

pop

it always puts a smile
on our faces
and then...
we let go

we let go

we see it
carried away
never
to return
up
up
up
till we can no longer
see it

and
we know
what will happen
to it

when it can't
go on any farther

when it can't
go on any further

ups/downs

I tell you
I'm having a nervous
break
DOWN

but
you said
UP
as you turned and walked away

now that was clever.

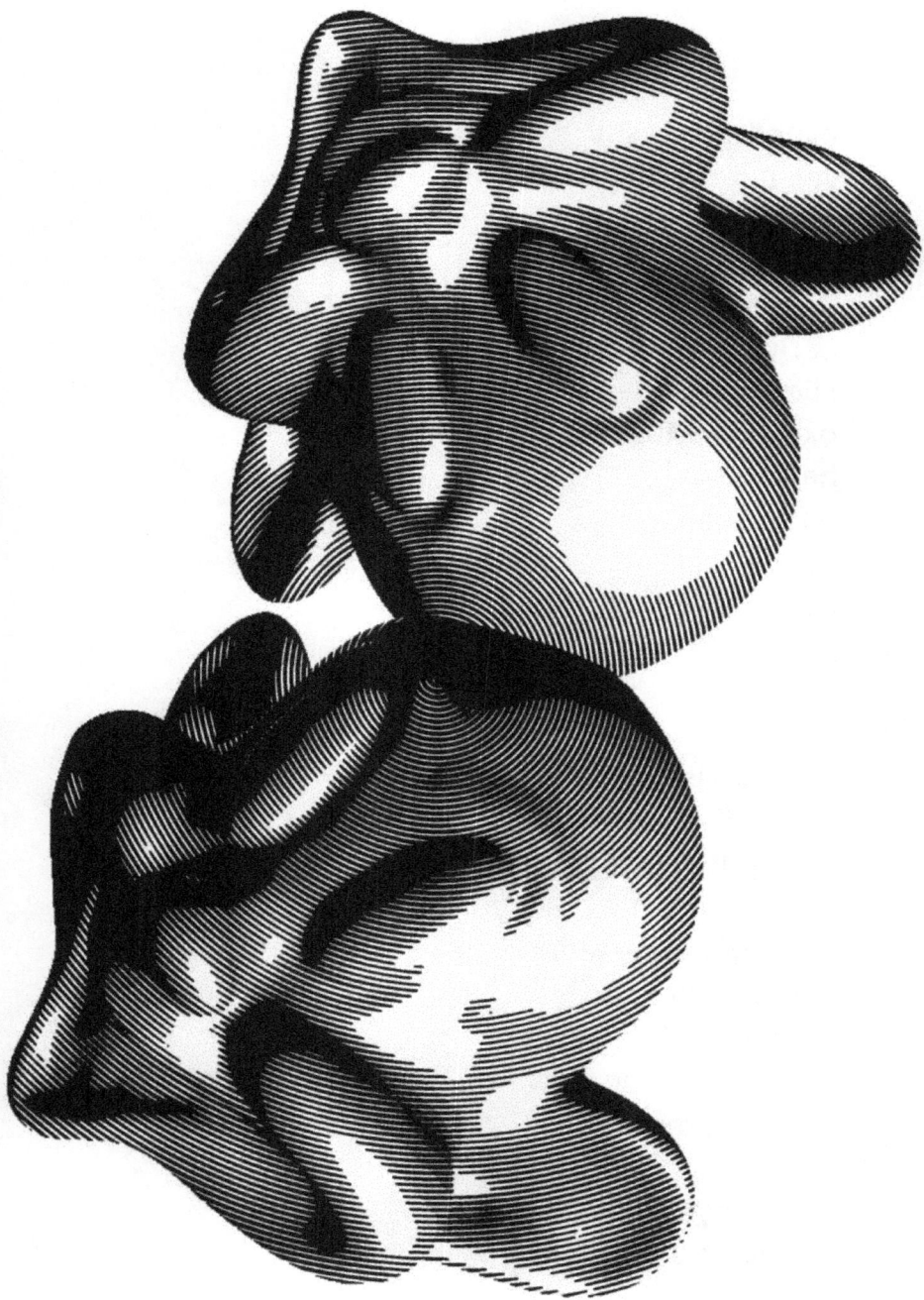

alone

everything is still
still not moving
a calm...
lazy night
but really
early morning
I lie awake
okay, I'm lying
half awake
half asleep
maybe
zoning off

not really

the television
full of life
giving the perception
that the room
is full of conversation
and participation
with flashes of light
spotlighting the floor
exposing the tile

but everything is still
still not moving

and I find myself
zoning off
when nothing is moving
but
everything becomes
broken up
interrupted
breaking the scene
controlling the scene
all...
out of the corner
of my eye
around the corner
from where I lie
it steadily moves
to where it catches
my eye
a spider
finding its spotlight
from the flashes of light
and
remains in position
till I give it
the recognition
it deserves

we are not alone

please be seated

when all else has
failed us
we still have
toilet seat covers
to protect us

you can bet your ass on it.

calculating the evolution of disappointment through the eyes of David Lynch

the gate is open

I left the gate
wide...open

and now
they will leave

they will all be...gone
         not to escape

just to...leave

in another direction
because it's different
because it's new
because it is simple

I can sleep at night
knowing

I have a conscience
and now
I am...conscious

I can hear you articulate
to me softly

"you were talking again...
in your sleep"

you roll back...over

i stare into...obscurity

and
remember

I left the gate open
wide...open.

know-it-all

I have found
at times
that my options
are limited

and at those times
which is most
of the time
I become more
creative
and
better at pretending
to have all the answers

this has limited me to
relying on my options

for dummies

this is not a love poem
do not be misguided.

But carry on
for transparency

this is
more
or less
is just another
do-it-yourself guide...
How to FEEL for Another

but we are all just dummies
and we have to be guided...
we have to be misguided

trained for free-thinking

but we can't hear ourselves think
when we talk over one another
and there will always be
too much static
without a referee

so
do-it-yourself...

this needs to be
ripped...released
from it's binding
and do-it-yourself

do with it what you will

actions
speak louder
than words

that is to FEEL.
that is how it is done.

dummy.

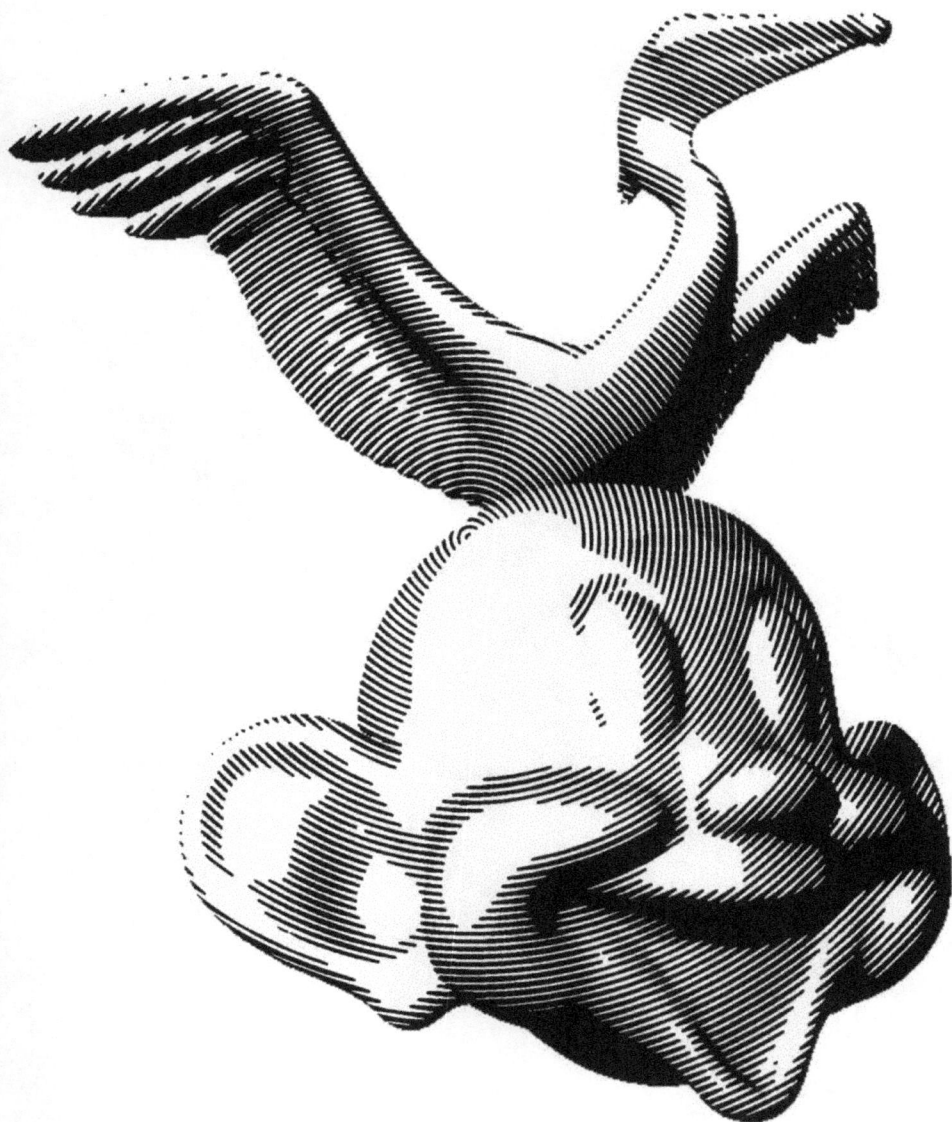

comprehending sanity

i've scratched my wrists
one too many times
two
three
4

and the scars are there
but you can't see them

like an etch-a-sketch
(shake)

like diarrhea in spandex

like knocking on a closet door

a symbolic preparation
for what is to come

i've answered your questions
(stupid questions)
in front of a drunken crowd
all in line
to shake my hand
(it's the shaking that has me concerned)

antibacterial soap cleanses

but it doesn't stop the shaking
it's cold here
in here
here by the door
two
three
four

visitation is over in 5

stalled

for a good time
call _____
at _____

and
who would
ever think
poetry
could be so
ruthless?

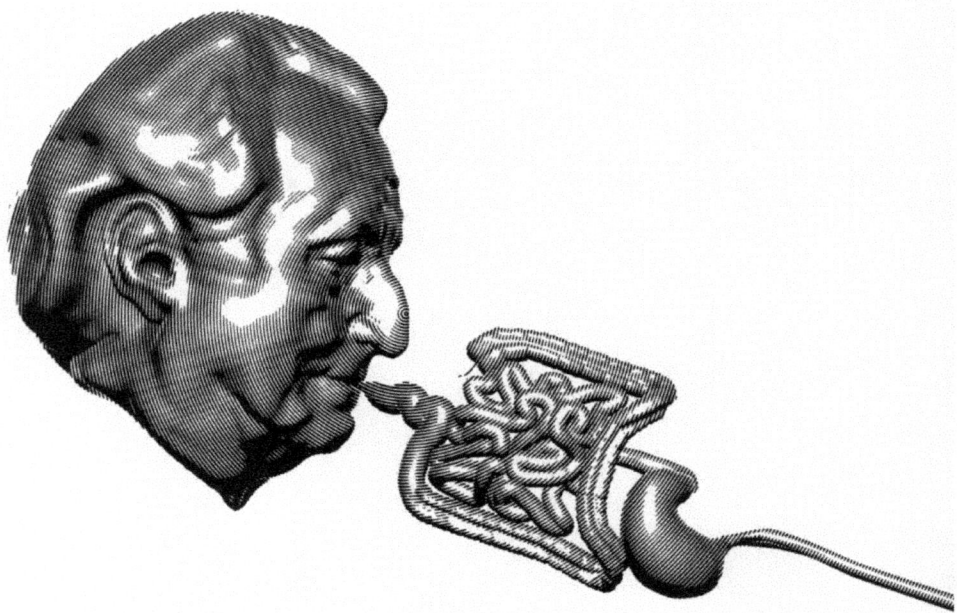

know time to waste

I stopped
to smell the flowers
but
there were too many
to smell
so
I bought
some more cologne

that is the only way
I could fit it in

night and day and yesterday

the remaining daylight
fades out with slight notice
and
superficial light
begins to highlight
significant areas
so we may continue
with whatever it is
we need to do

we've put time in place
to control the night
as much as the day

and as scheduled...
night has fallen
and we have become
less essential
swallowed by infinity...

reminding us
we aren't so intelligent
no matter what we think we know

the stars begin to unfold themselves
exploited Lite Brite pictures
that we have labeled

believing we can own their creations

but
we are foolish...
no matter what we've accomplished
it will never be enough
if we can't take care of what we already
have

how can we paint the sky
the universe
when we can't see the big picture
just what is in front of us
there is more depth to what we see

but then again, who am I fooling
we've proven we don't have such great
depth perception
our last greatest feat...was discovering
the world wasn't flat

after that, we just consumed space and
call it how we see it

hearing impaired

I am nobody

(nonetheless)
intended for
none of the less

but rationally speaking
more of the none

because
that's forever...especially
when there is no value

and with just one word
(all or nothing)
I'll show you
that
I'll have it
no other way...

rest assured
I'll beat you
at your own game
but
you whine...
then dine with me
and over pleasant

conversation

you say
"it's not fair when you don't make any sense"
and I...
I calmly reply
with all respect
"don't listen when I have nothing to say"

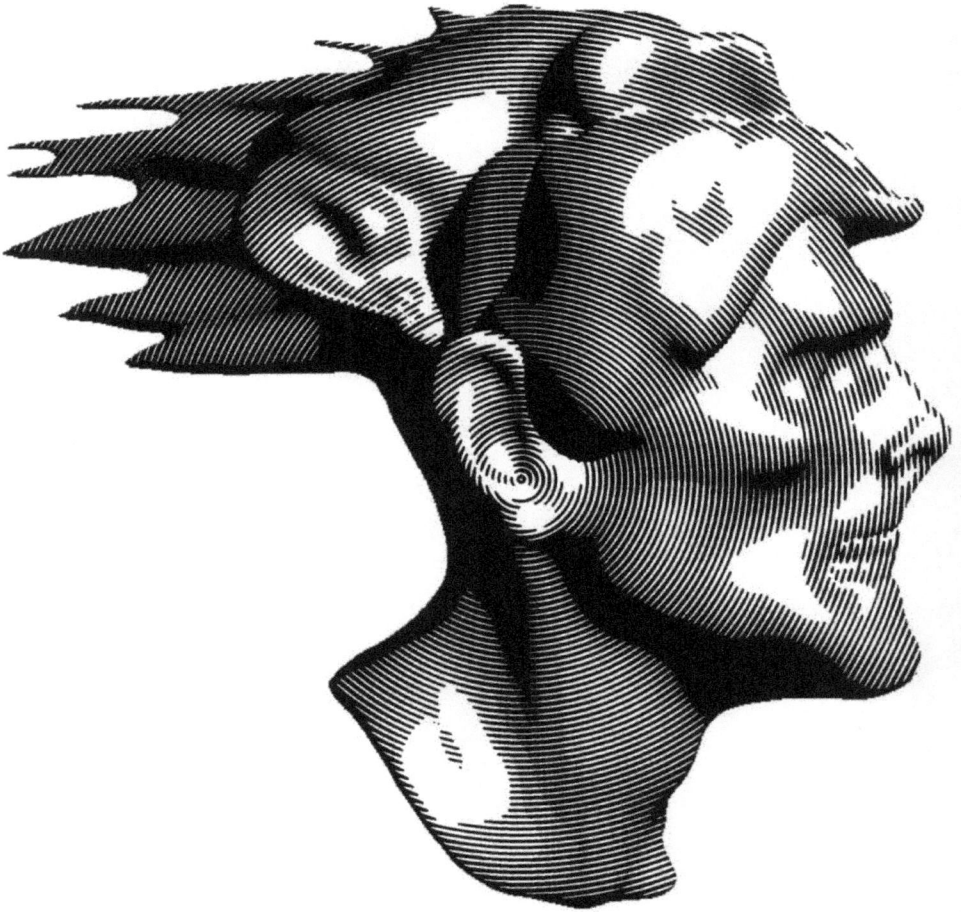

successful

I was never meant
to be
but

to be
a b-side

and
I will take
seconds
and
restore
what little
confidence
you may have
in me
and
show you
at least
I know people
and
some people
know me

surviving

thank you
for continuing to hold.

we are experiencing
a large volume
of calls at this time.

your call
will be answered
in the order
it was received.

please continue to hold
and the next
representative
will assist you.

shortly.

limited warranty

expiration dates
get in the way
of magic

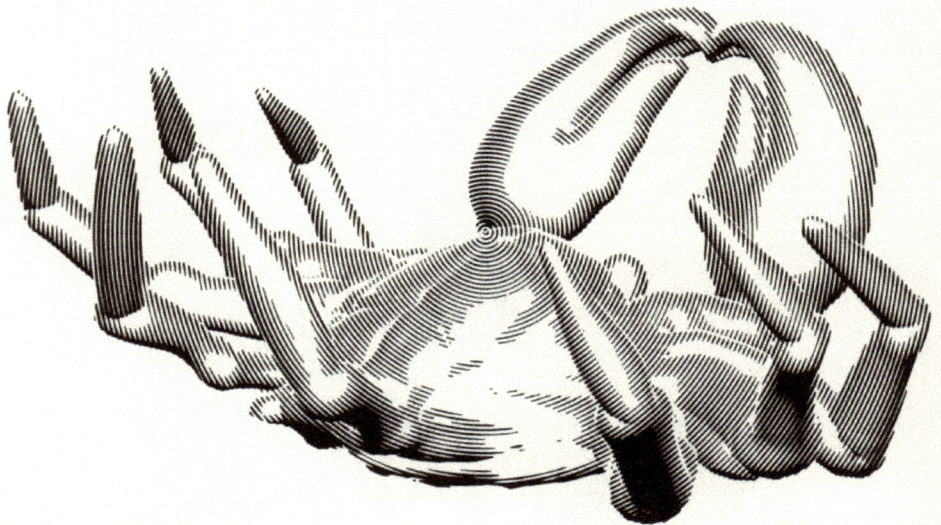

and now a word from our sponsor

I dealt with being scared
at an age when I couldn't spell it
S-C-A-R-R-E-D
and I was that too
but
I could spell my name just fine
on Styrofoam cups
in GREAT BIG LETTERS
but
they were never mine
they were disposable
like me

I dealt with constant change
at an age when I required stability
our only address
was an address book
filled with names, numbers and streets...
but
it was more like a log book
CAPTAIN'S LOG STARDATE
crossing out where we had been
and circling our possible destinations
Xs and Os aren't always kisses and hugs
and exploring new frontiers
isn't as exciting
and glamorous

as Hollywood makes it out to be

I dealt with being alone
at an age when I had to create a world
"you got the whole world in your hands"
not really
that's childish... tricks are for kids
the world was too big for LITTLE hands
the world was too life-size for me
but I still played the games
like
the game of LIFE
the game of RISK
but
those weren't really games
SORRY!
that wasn't a game either

(INTERMISSION)

AND NOW
A WORD FROM OUR SPONSOR

"Are you having trouble dealing with anxiety,
change and depression?
Well I have the solution for you
and it's all in this blue pill!
Trust me; all your troubles will end"

AND NOW
BACK TO OUR PROGRAMMING

I dealt with too many interruptions
and paid advertisements
telling me what I NEED
to make me happy...happy

I dealt with having to need insurance
when all I needed was assurance

I dealt with trends and tabloids
gossip and bullies
addictions and excuses

I dealt with having to deal
having to cope
having to have
having to be me

all at an age when I could recognize the bullshit

2nd job

these are
part-time words
employed by me
to come through
for me
when I have nothing
beneficial
to write about

when I'm distracted
repeatedly

I need the help
part-time help
to piece together
a thought

but it's still minimum wage

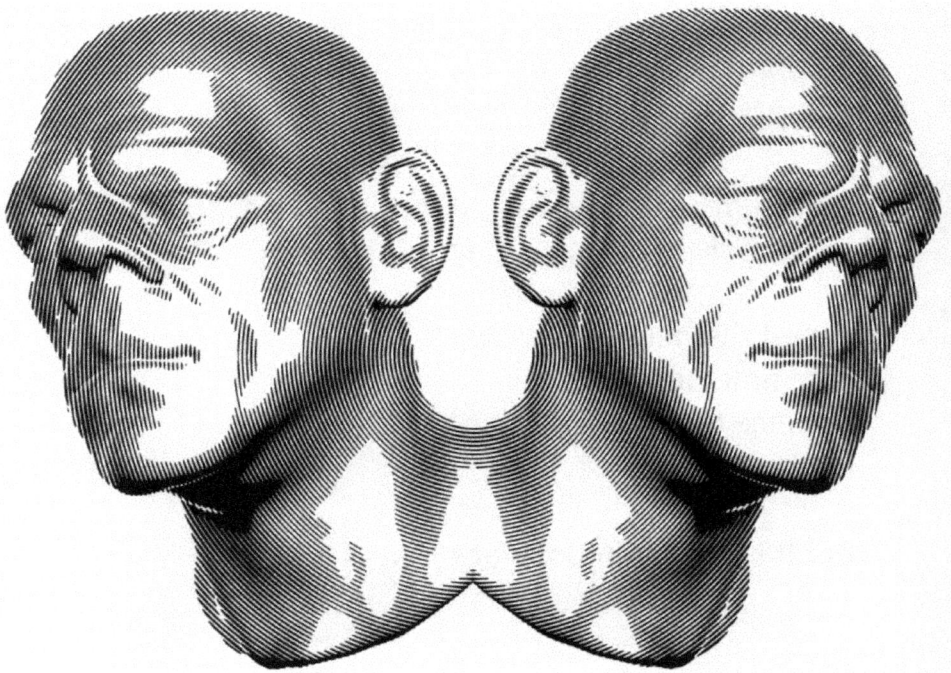

writer's block (to be cont'd)

quantity is quality.

BEWARE: uninvited attention

we have become amateurs
in our dialogue
mimicking commercials
and poorly written scripts.
an overmedicated generation
correlated with reality television
and zombie flicks
(and we all know zombies
like to eat brains...think about it)

this is our newfound culture
ill-mannered and unaware
an infectious disaster
of redundancy spotlighted
by the latest celebrity downfall.

this is our newfound plague
recycling effective communication
to abuse and reuse
for another unwanted discussion.
BUT
"It's only $19.99 and if you act now..."

we rely on the media
and dying art
to tell us what we need to know
to spoon feed

our thought processes
and our passions for trends

we have been outwitted by ourselves
creating technologies
to mask our interactions
to subdue our fears
to hide behind prepackaged belief systems,
helpless reruns and daytime talk shows

these are our foretold distractions
and we have nothing to...

EXCUSE ME
I have to take this call...

hallelujah!

redemption...
all spelled out
and
here for the taking
so
take a number

hopefully

you won't be overlooked
or
misplaced

that happens...you know
to people who wait

but

take a number

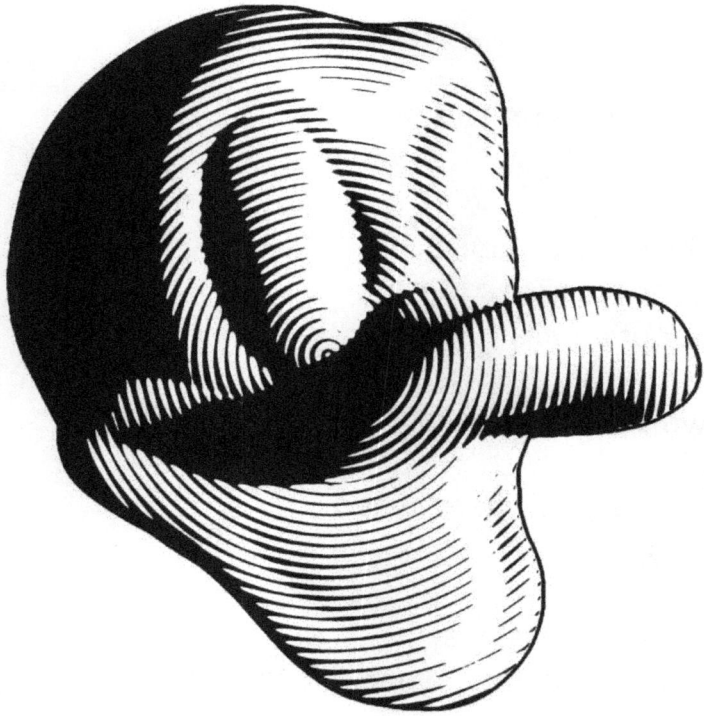

that is the question

what you don't know
can't hurt you
and
the general public
doesn't know a thing
about details

we don't know a thing
about
who, what, where, when
why

it's easier that way...
believing there are enough band-aids
to go around for everyone
But
we have been exhausted
and now
OUT OF ORDER

we are left to
fogive and to forget

to remain SILENT
(with a chip on our shoulders)

to blame ourselves

for avoiding ourselves

and
to realize...
we didn't ask enough questions...
the right question

to be or not to be?

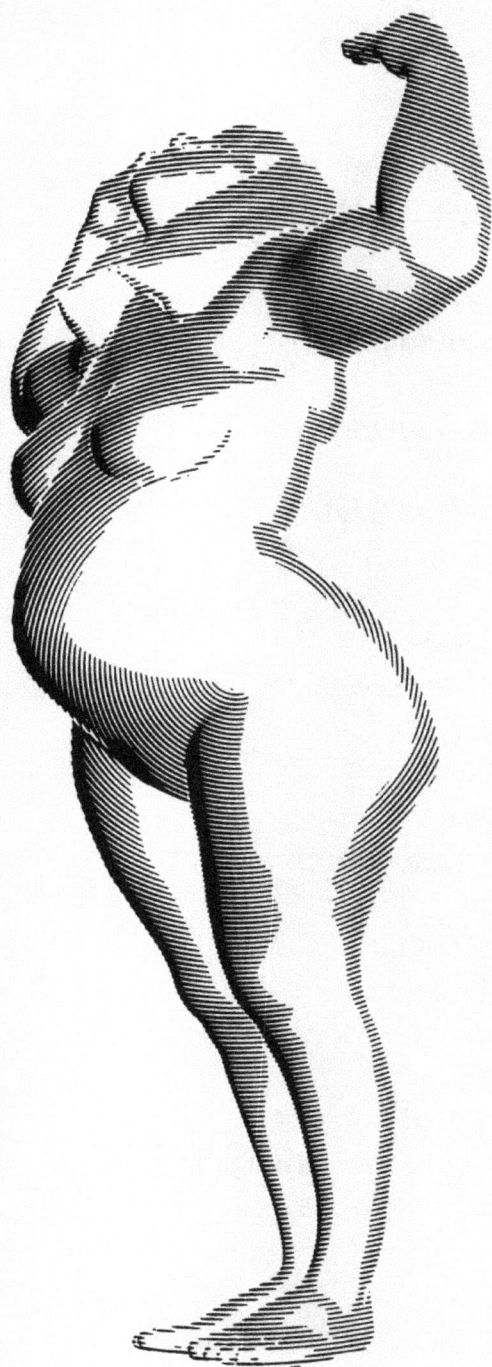

www.whenhewouldsnapagain.com

eeny, meeny, miny, moe
catch a tiger by the toe
if he hollers

(and he would holler)

then make him pay

(but we would pay)

and
find ourselves
escaping him
once again

always with
a trail of breadcrumbs
left behind
for him to find us
each and everytime
and it didn't take long for me
to realize
that she could not let go
that he would make things great
again...just for awhile

and I was...

waiting
watching
wondering
whenhewouldsnapagain
dot
com

and this time
I would find a way
to get away
and make her pay
each and everyday

she made the decision
to catch the tiger

governed

I plead the 5th
a vow of silence

organized religion

an oxymoron
for you to laugh about

but who really cares
anymore?

this was never meant
to go this far

but

it's trendy

Welcome *to the* APPLEPARROT HALFTIME SPECIAL

featuring

Carey Bell

and

August Edwards

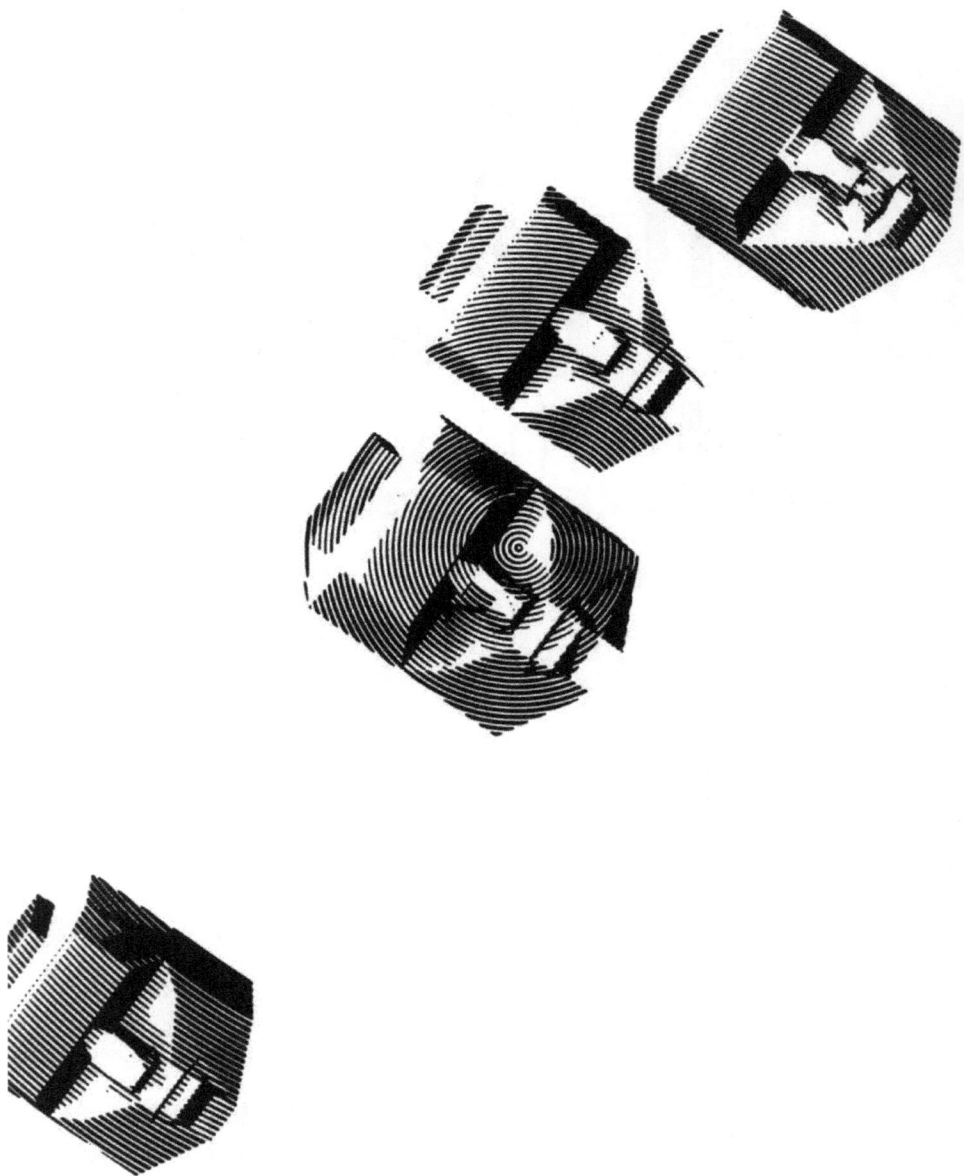

Carey Bell

HOTPAD

Is it hot in here,
Or is it just my hand?

Screams deafening
Intense pain and a smell

A smell of flesh burning

The odor makes me want to vomit
Cold water and ice

Pain is gone for a moment
Scarred for life

Carey Bell

TIMELAPSE

Such a slow process

Turn on the heat
The water flows

The pan is heavy

Now you wait

And wait

And wait some more
Finally it is time

Open the door
Where are they?
Don't tell me...

Damn, it's empty

August Edwards

Ghosts

Ghosts will always come
For acts we've done in the past
I know my ghost's name

Helping

Let's help each other
Find someone you can work with
I always choose me

Somewhere

Being somewhere great
Is like being somewhere bad
What do you expect?

Heaven Forbid

Heaven forbid, that,
You get hit by a truck
And I cry a lake

Super Bowl

Super Bowl show down
Football match between two teams
Only one will win

Inspirations

Inspirations come
They also play hide-and-seek
Keep looking for them

Water

Cascading water
Rippling through a fountain spout
From the bathroom sink

Groundhog Day

Groundhog Day is here
Let's make him find his shadow
Put a hat on him

Differences

Differences come
They fly and say look at me
Let's all accept them

Puppet

Mr. Monkey Head
Entertains and provides laughs
My lovely puppet

August Edwards

AppleParrot
HALFTIME SPECIAL

Guilt

Guilt fills your body
Fills your heart with great sadness
Hope for forgiveness

Television Blues

Television blues
Limited channel supply
Well, let's write instead

Collecting

Collecting items
Helps you build up interests
But why collect stamps?

Humor

Humor's good to have
In awkward situations
I've used many times

Where You're From

Think of where you're from
Greatly appreciate it
Then get out of there

Going Away

You're going away?
You've gotten tired of me?
Alright, off you go

Entitled

Entitled to choice
Entitled to opinions
Entitled to live

Laughing Out Loud

I'm laughing out loud
No, it's not because of your joke
You have no humor

Balloons

Balloons: flexible
Choose when to inflate or die
Let's all be a balloon

Food

Food you can't reuse
You can't use food to clean things
Food is excrement

August Edwards

Quarreling

Quarreling madness
Hurting people who differ
Shake your head in shame

Scientist

Save yourself, get out
I'm experimenting here
I'm a scientist

Sellable

Make sellable things
Make sure people will buy them
Bring some money in

Fake

Storytelling is
Diff'rent from fortune telling
But they're both fake fun

Warren Zevon R.I.P

Little old lady
Mutilated late last night
Werewolves of London

Push-Pins

Push-pins are useful
To push things into the wall
But hurt to sit on

Activia

Activia helps
Keep old ladies regular:
Jamie Lee Curtis

Pens

Pens are not pencils
Pens make all of your mistakes
You need erasers

Shoes

Shoes don't like their job
Always walking and scuffing
They're very tired

You Ask

You just don't know who
Warren Zevon is, well you're
Not hip to Sev'nties

August Edwards

Softball

Softball conundrum:
It is a sport for young girls
And beer-drinking men

Zoo-Free

Lions and bears
Tigers, penguins, and giraffes
Want to be zoo-free

Stuck Song

I just hate it when
There is a song in my head
And can't get it out

Funny

I am so funny
But, now that I think of it
Only I think that

Return of the Fly

James, help! I'm a bee!
Actually, you're a fly,
And my name's not James

The Disaster Gift

Oh, aren't you so nice?
You got a present for me?
What's that ticking sound...

Stronger

When one is standing still
And one swims against currents
Which will get stronger?

10:34

Macaulay Culkin
Whatever happened to him?
Is he still alone?

12:13

So many road kills
Think how these animals feel
And how we drive off

2:20

Once we were driving
I just wanted to look up
And I saw bird poop

August Edwards

Tick, Tock, Tick

Time is ticking by
You can hear it, tick, tock, tick
Get that damn clock out!

Ask Alice

Somebody tell me…
How is a little raven
Like a writing desk?

Praying for End

People love parties
They dance, play games, and goof off
I pray for the end

New York Times

I'm gonna' be great
Number one with a bullet
The Times' bestseller

AND NOW
BACK TO OUR PROGRAMMING

bitter: bar of soap

I have developed
a profane vocabulary
over the years
and
a bar of soap
in the mouth
has
left me to
speak in tongues

blah
blah
blah
and blah!

a bar of soap
the temporary
resolution for the pollution

a punishment
with
a bitter aftertaste
and
I know some
sign language
but
I have dirty hands

and signing with
dirty hands
is just as profane

a bar of soap
for a dirty mouth
a bar of soap
for these dirty hands

employees must
wash hands before
returning to work

here's a middle finger for you

may I take your order?

you have the right

FREEZE!
now...
SPREAD THEM!

this is hardcore
this is WHAT to expect
but
STOP!
WAIT!
let's not get ahead of ourselves
just for a moment
but please
take a moment
to think about it...

when you are all alone
with your opinion
and
taste is left to reckon with
you'll find yourself alone
and feel...alone
with guilty pleasures

but then
you snap out of it
and
reason with yourself

that you are innocent till
proven guilty

and then
you realize
that you still have a price to pay
and you can't afford
a good lawyer

justice is served

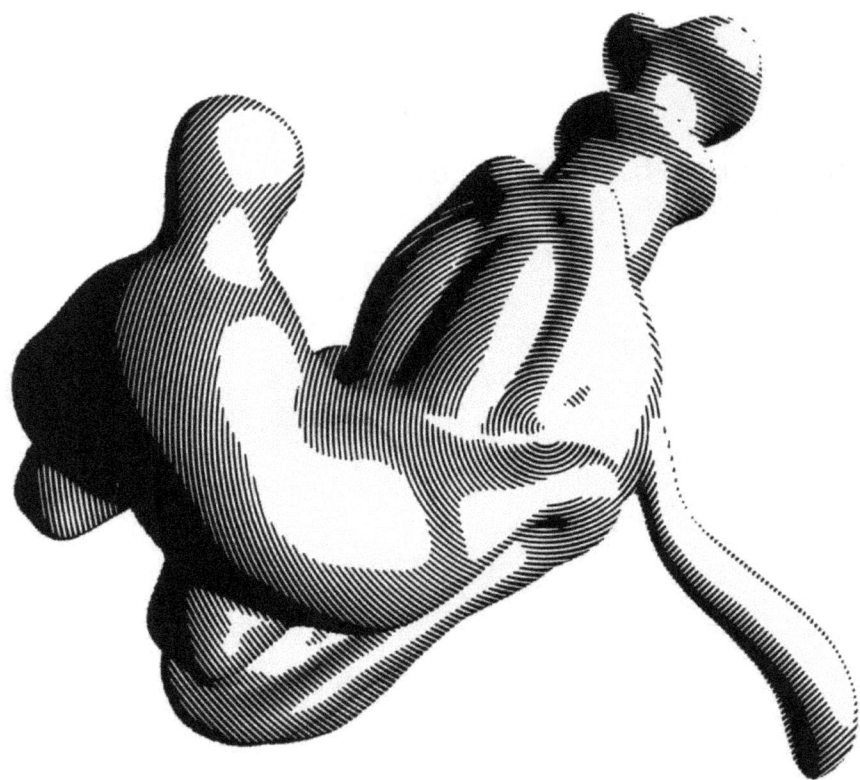

wants

ring the bell
for
service

and maybe
just maybe

you will be heard

just be prepared
to state
what you NEED

it's not as simple
as
ringing the bell

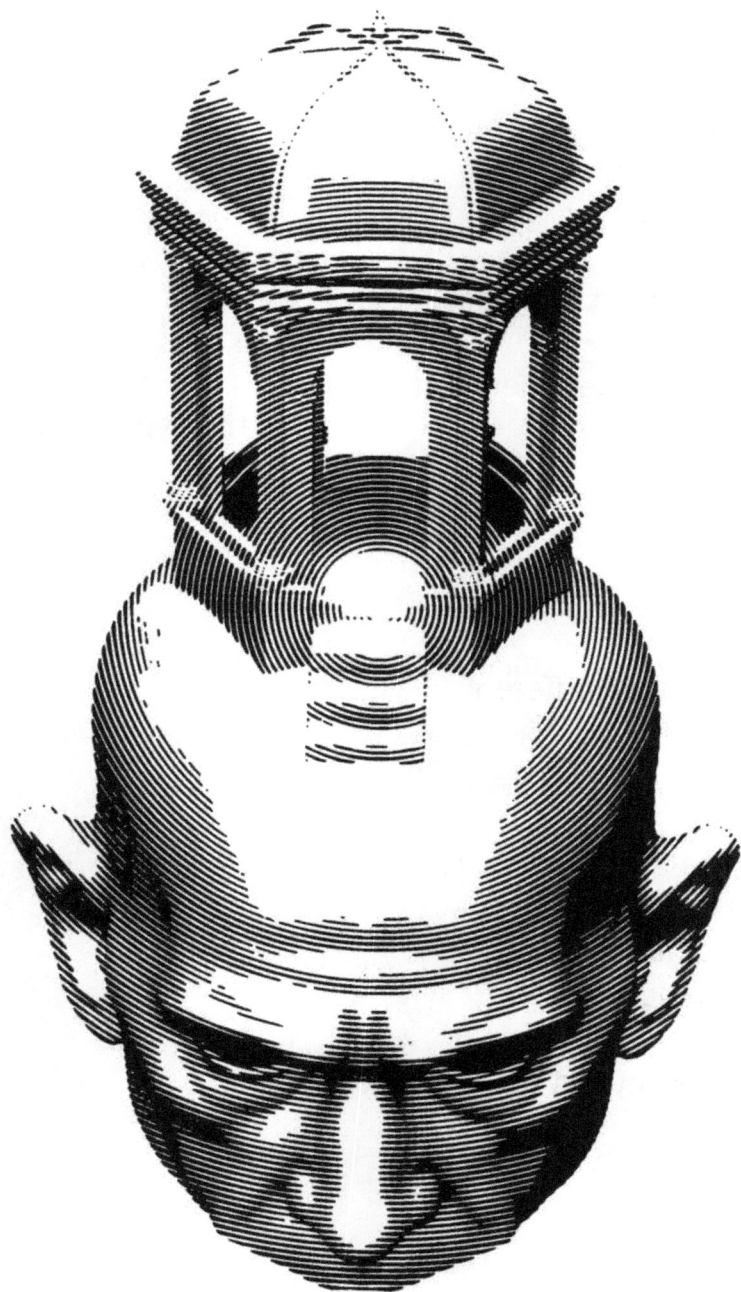

flashback

I can see
around me
nothing

but simplicity

impregnated memorabilia

passing the eye

familiar

but

things are different

now

I can see what I have missed

and now
it is too late

this is my last roll of film...
snap

and
flash

and now

I can only wait

wait

wait

wait for it all to develop

I will never capture it all again.

created a monster

these are my
concluding words
to
what is said
further down
this page
further down
as
you
read

and

furthermore
as you see
that I am important
and

hopefully

you'll
comprehend
that I have
been trying
very
very
hard

to create
and leave
behind
an idea
further down
this page

further down
this page

but then
you realize

I am

wasting space
and your
hard-earned time

this is me confessing
to you

I don't know
where to begin
no matter if
I've already
started.

stopwatch

we don't take time
the time
to prepare anything
for anything
because it's inconvenient
so we have others
do the stuff
we don't have time
the time for
and we spend time
more time
finding faster
a faster way
to make time
more time
that we don't have
to offer
but at the end of it all
at the end of the day
everyday
we find that we never
never keep up with ourselves
and it becomes redundant
redundant.

a moment of silence

chance

a crime seen/do not cross

what my eyes have seen
a crime scene
chalked in pastels
outlined
an exhibition
that drew our attention.

we avoided
the tape...
investigating
the familiar ground
where we drew silly faces
played hopscotch
and shared an addiction
that wasn't ours.

we were just kids
defying authority
for curiosity
in search of
an explanation
but the grown-ups...

it was all make-believe.

and so we found
ourselves shielded

by innocence

foolish
believing that evil things
happen to others
that nothing bad
could never

ever

happen to us.

we were just kids.

dirty work

I have found
Janitor Services
in the
Yellow Pages

See Also House Cleaning
Maids' & Butlers' Services

but
it all just seems too easy

a price to pay
when we can't clean up
our own mess

but
I can't afford
these *services*
so
I'll continue
to be
responsible
for my own mess
for my own actions

Donnie Darko

Where is Donnie?

...little hostile there

Maybe

You should be the one
in therapy
then
mom and dad
can pay someone
$200 an hour
to listen to all your thoughts
so
we don't have to.

Do you want tell
mom and dad
why
you stop taking
your medication?

Where do you go at night?

What happened to my son?

I don't recognize this person today.

Then
why don't you start taking
the goddamn pills?

Wake up.

I've been
watching you.

Come closer.
Closer...

That is when the world will end.

Why?

evolution

sex sells
sales
sails

cells.

free will

this is
not
so strange

but
how do you feel
about it?

exorcised
exercised

I no longer
need training
wheels

medically speaking

pharmacies
are
putting
crack houses

out of business

and

this

is just a
side effect

please be
patient

a patient

something there

I have been doing nothing
and nothing
has been going on

BUT
because of nothing
there will always
be something...

that something
we will need
when we need it
the most

do you follow?

of course you do
and everybody
knows best...
creating a name
for that something

BUT
to me it is still
just nothing
and that...
is clear to me.

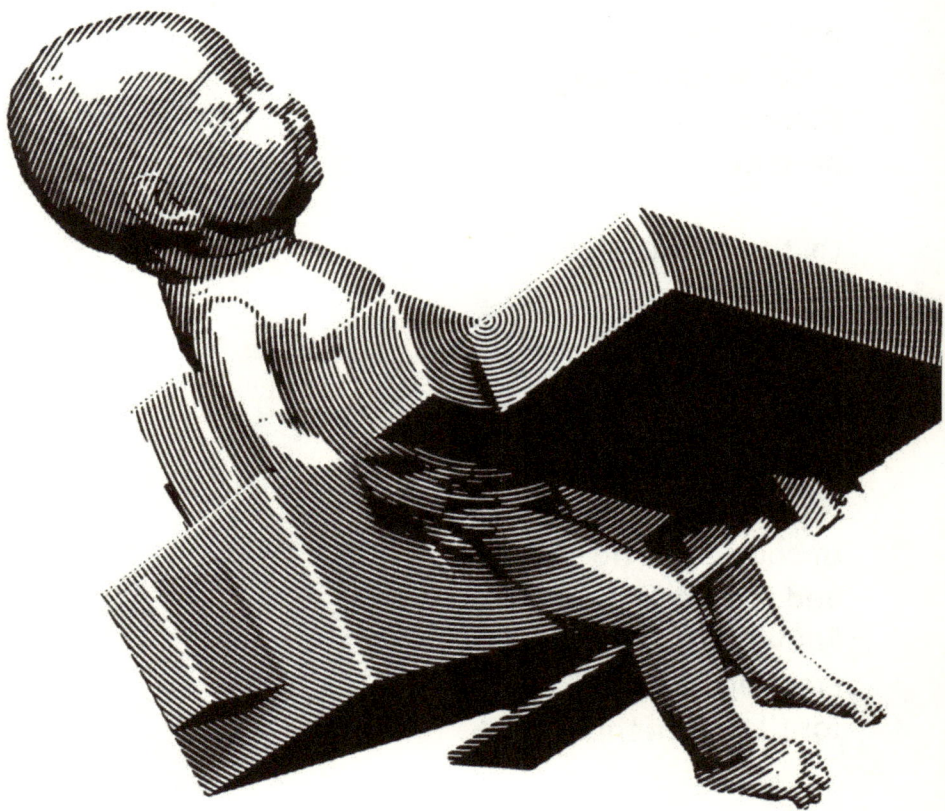

thou shalt not...

this was meant
to be
thrown away

thrown
out the window

but

I did not
want to litter

because
I'm not a litterbug

and
THAT

makes me a
better person

but

you can throw this
away

out the window

and

I will not judge you

even if...
that makes me a
better person

but

who am I to judge?

you now have the floor

all the world's a stage

the jokes on you

and
the audience is in on it
ha, ha, ha...

really?

I'm preaching to the choir

because
they really didn't know
that that
was your plan
all along
with your countless one-liners
and
cheap smiles
it was all just a diversion
to help make them
think
that that
you were just a fool
and that you were beneath
them

and
that, that
is what they need to feel
good about themselves
to feel better than you

lol

but
I'm not laughing

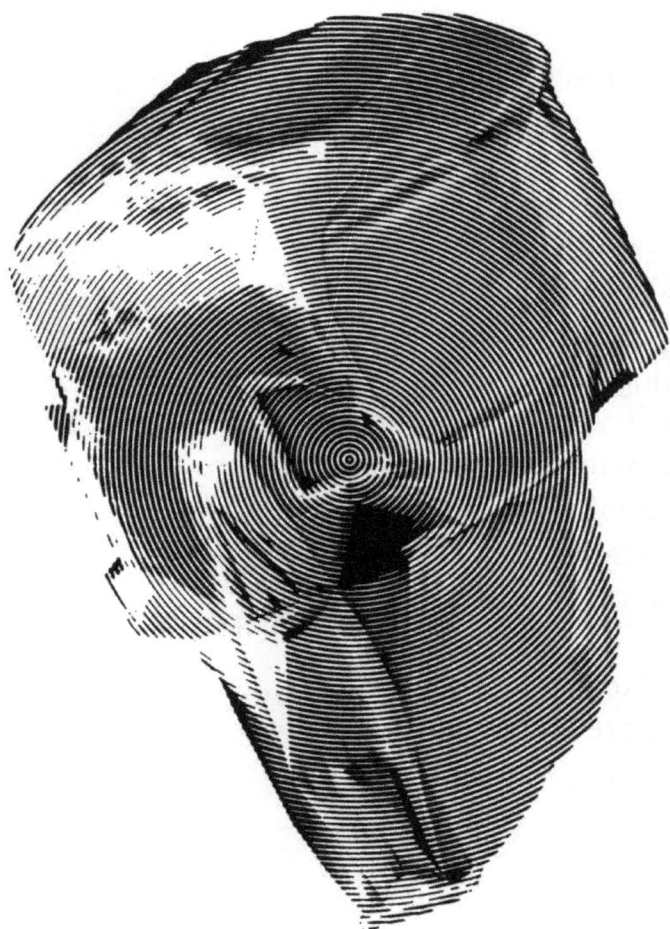

piñata

I'm a bit scattered
all over the place
like the cheap plastic toys
and expired candy
lying in every direction

tied up and beaten
by everyone
a line of acquaintances
taking the opportunity
to swing
(swing batter batter)
as I'm helpless
predictably swaying
and decaying
caving in

and all that remains
is a before and after
picture, physical presence
of what I was
who I was
and
everything inside me
is gone, gutted
exposed
exploited

and scattered

all that is left of me
is worthless

like
cheap plastic toys
and expired candy

We the People: take your medicine

a spoonful of sugar
helps the medicine
go down
but
what if...
We the People
don't want to take
the medicine.
let's not sugarcoat
the situation...
the cliché filled trickeries
sales pitches
consume the consumer
and
We the People
have become consumed.
we've become critics
analyzing the presentation
more than product.
We the People
are more enticed
by the idea
of secured contentment
and
pretty faces
and
handsome grins

telling us
selling us
to take the
pharmaceutical antidote
because they know
what is best for us.
We the People
are left to be sold
on critically acclaimed diversions
on the possibility
of liver failure.
kidney failure.
failure...
of every important organ
that...
We the People
rarely consider...
taking it all for granted
because
We the People
didn't worry
about the possible
side effects...
focusing more on convenience
the commercial
the ad
showcasing
the idea of bestowing
the perfect life again
because
We the People

are ignorant to believe
in living a normal life
being normal
and all of the
animated happiness
foretold by
pretty faces
and
handsome grins
overshadowing
the fine print
but it's all okay
Because
We the People
don't pay attention
to the fine print
just immediate happiness
the slogans
the catchy phrases
the jingles
proving
a little sugar
can coat the situation
any situation
every situation
but none of this matters
because...
We the People
will remain in
our oblivious state
holding each

other's hand
and in perfect harmony...
We the People
will sing...
just a spoonful of sugar
helps the medicine
go down...

in a most delightful way.

parking lot masquerade

we approach the night
with our own petty agendas
engaging in networks
of communication
and
impersonating
absurd references
that we had been exposed to
from the last eight hours

a small, coveted radius
of over-produced clubs
and smoke-filled bars
down a long, vintage strip
swallowed by parking lots
endless cars that are now
vacated and forgotten

we approach the night
to linger in our own
parking lot, our own
drive-in theater
all for the entertainment
of others who sell their morals
for one-night stands,
cascading filled beers
and specialty drinks

that bartenders
all make differently

this is where we belong
our own parking lot
our hideaway
clearly subdued
with no association
with no affiliation
watching carefully
each and every
patron marching by
on a one-way street
in both directions
carelessly contributing
to the tattooed street
that has a history of being
tormented by production
abused by escapades
a sober mind
could not designate

these patrons of the night
these walking billboards
mistakenly have
everything to sell
purposely
nothing to lose
and everything to gain
spilling their
performances in front

of a careless crowd
laughing, crying, screaming,
and not saying a word
but they are all clowns
with graffiti-painted faces
and inexcusable hair
falling upon each other
stumbling
to be caught
to be rescued
to save any false hope
feeling that they are alive
and everything else
is dead, irrelevant
lifeless without the party

and we
take it all in
give it all away
knowing we are nothing
without the masquerade
and so, again

we approach the night

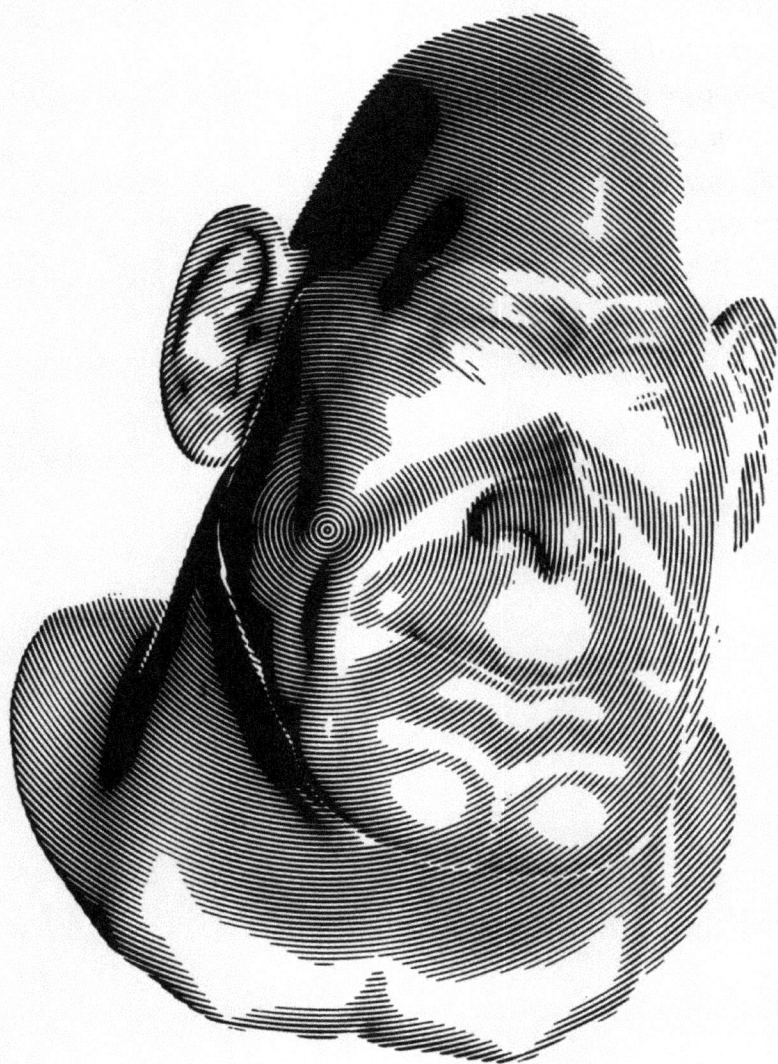

Basquiat

SAMO
as an end
to bogus pseudo
intellectual.
My mouth, therefore
an error.
Plush safe...
he think.

R. Mutt

hey champ

I miss the urinal
on occasion

but
can find
consistency
in my
readymade mess.

starving artist

rich text format

the economy has left me
with just enough
spare change
to coin a new word
or phrase
but

I'm saving it for
a wishing well

or just
a fountain
that is located
in a mall
where all the
big spenders
flaunt what they don't have

or maybe
I'll just return home
and save what sense (cents)
I have left
to create art
that none of us can afford.

BONUS FEATURE

Films are remade and music is covered. The poetic attribute we find in originality is lost in reproduction.

Therefore, I have decided to cover an Edgar Allan Poe poem, attempting to reproduce originality poetically based on this concept.

Please Stay Tuned...

Edgar Allan Poe's

Alone

covered by Cory Allen

From childhood's hour I have not been
As others were; I have not seen
As others saw; I could not bring
My passions from a common spring.
From the same source I have not taken
My sorrow; I could not awaken
My heart to joy at the same tone;
And all I loved, I loved alone.
Then- in my childhood, in the dawn
Of a most stormy life- was drawn
From every depth of good and ill
The mystery which binds me still:
From the torrent, or the fountain,
From the red cliff of the mountain,
From the sun that round me rolled
In its autumn tint of gold,
From the lightning in the sky
As it passed me flying by,
From the thunder and the storm,
And the cloud that took the form
(When the rest of Heaven was blue)
Of a demon in my view.

Special Thanks
to
Daniel Edwards, Amber Losson, Carey Bell, and August Edwards
for making *Maybe* complete.

and to
My Family and Friends
who have supported me through all my endeavors.
You all will always be the reason I succeed.

www.ingramcontent.com/pod-product-compliance
Lightning Source LLC
Chambersburg PA
CBHW051834040426
42447CB00006B/529